The Angel Poetry Collection

Rachelle Rose

Table of Contents

Hope & Healing
The Year For Healing 4
The Angel Within Me 6
.... 7
The Angel Within You 8
Always Be Kind 9
The Truth About Me 10
Rapunzel Revisited 11
Alone 12
Grieve 13
Heartache 14
To Thy Own Self Be True 15
Live For The Moment 16
Today 17

Life & Love
Angel Dance 20
Miracles 21
Dream 22
Beautiful 23
The Embrace 24
Quite Like That 25
An Honorable Man 26
By God's Grace 28

Motherhood
The Perfect Mother 30
Queen Mom 31
Ode To My Life 32
My Little Angel ~ Arielle Nina ~ May 12th 1988 33
Wish On A Star ~ Johnathan Anthony ~ April 6th 1990 34
Sealed With A Kiss ~ Brett Matthew ~ February 5th 1993 35
Sweet Little Beaner Boo ~ Serena Rose ~ July 6th 1994 36
Last But Not Least ~ Michael Edward ~ September 7th 1995 .. 37

Just For Fun
Twinkle Twinkle 39
The Snow Day 42

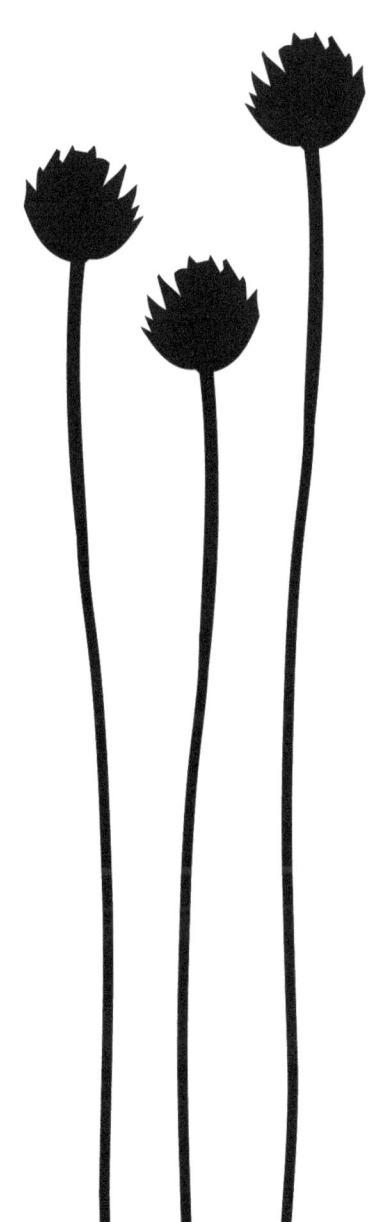

Angels whisper to my heart
things I need to know
words of hope and wisdom
to help me heal and grow
I'm guided by their gentle force
to write these thoughts divine
and pass them on in love and light
to all of humankind

Rachelle Rose

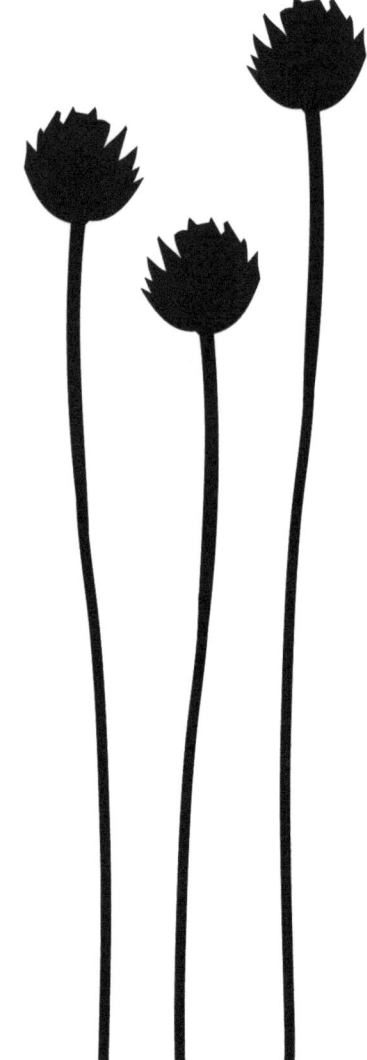

Love heals all things!

ative, negatively-val # Hope & Healing

and so
it will be...

The Year For Healing

Let this be the year for healing
especially our hearts
Bestow on us your awesome grace
as you have right from the start

Wash away our judgments
and remind us who we are:
beautiful tender spirits
in a world that's all too hard

A world that's filled with hardship
weighing on our souls
A world where many suffer
and have no place to go

A world that tells us lies
and tricks us into greed
that turns us on each other
when love is all we need

Help us give forgiveness
and lift each other high
Through tender words and kindness
wipe the tears we all may cry

Let this be the year for healing
together help us grow
to a place of peace and comfort
where love is all we know

AMEN

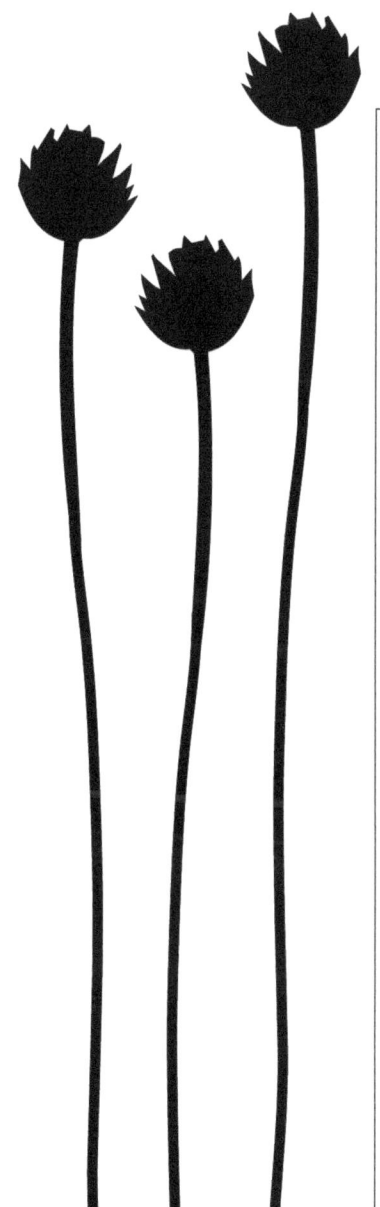

"In love and in dreams there are no impossibilities"

Janos Arany

The Angel Within Me

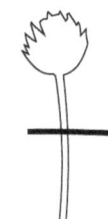

Deep amidst the darkness
beneath the shadowy plains
I know there lies an angel in me
buried by all of life's pain

Her wings they must be broken
she's been missing for sometime
I can barely remember her presence
before her soul was broken from mine

As I sift through all of life's rubble
searching for a sign
I hear her voice call out to me
it sounds a lot like mine

Then I see her arms reached out
to far for me to hold
In her eyes I see the past
stories left untold

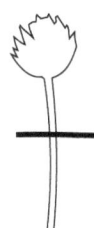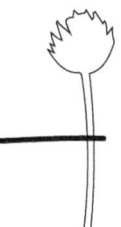

Her stories were filled with sorrow
old wounds that never healed
I saw why my angel had stepped aside
when the fears of my life were so real

She left me not to hurt me
rather trying to save my soul
For with her she kept a piece of my heart
so that nothing could hurt me in whole

I held out my arms to my angel
slowly we became one
Then with all my strength I faced my past
no longer will I run

I have found the angel within me
Once again I am whole
Now that we are together
I can heal and love and grow

The Angel Within You

The rain pours down from big gloomy clouds
in the end producing life
the trees and plants and beauty
Creation....

In life you weather many storms
with each one learning more
Even when it feels destructive
know it has formed the person you are
and the knowledge you have
It has given you strength
Beauty...

If no one else ever sees this beauty
it does not really matter
for you are your own angel made just for you
discovering the power you have within
Spirit...

When prayers seem hopeless and unfulfilled
just remember, you are not forgotten
for you have your inner self
The Angel Within You...

Let your angel fly!

Always Be Kind

We do not see the forest through the trees
Until autumn has shed its camouflage leaves

We do not see the movement
of the creatures in the night
Until winters soft snowfall
brings their footprints to sight

We do not see the wonder
of them wet dreary days
Until spring has sprung flowers
while butterflies play

We do not see the beauty
of earth's lovely land
Until summers warmth touches
the landscape so grand

We do not see the power
of one simple kind deed
Until one is bestowed
upon us when in need

We do not see the hurt another may feel
But our kindness may just help that person to heal

So Always be kind!

The Truth About Me

These secrets I'm keeping nobody knows
The depths of my struggles are locked in my soul
I'd give you the key and I'd let you come in
But I know I can't trust you, there's no one I can

I've trusted before and I've seen where that's led
Pictures are painted then tear drops are shed
So I'll go it alone so safely I'll be
No one quite knowing the truth about me

The truth about me, I wanna be free
Free from these fears that I carry with me
Maybe it's time that the truth guides my way
You're only as sick as your secrets they say

I'd finish this song if I knew how it goes
Not much to say when the truth is untold
God send me an angel a friend that I know
I promise I'll share from the depths of my soul

These secrets I've buried inside for so long
Then I'll pick up my pen and I'll finish this song

let down your hair...

Rapunzel Revisited

Long and lush golden hair
Fell across her face
Over her shoulders and down her back
It softly and lavishly raced

Long enough to nervously twirl
Hidden and safe it kept this girl

One day he forbid her to cut it
As he felt he could rightly say
So she had to finally honor herself
Her hair was gone the very next day

She felt naked and exposed
Yet a new found pride arose

Although she loved her long golden locks
Her hair is kept short to this day
To remind her that she belongs to herself
And no one can take that away

UPDATE:
Some years have past and this girl has grown
Now a strong willed woman with a mind of her own
She left that man and with a dream and a prayer
she opened a coffee shop and is growing her hair

Alone

Time alone to honor me
To heal ~ To grow ~ To be okay
To find my way
Alone
Sorting memories
Going slow
Acknowledging where I've been
And therefore where I'll go
Bonding with friends
Old and new
Being true to myself in all I do
Not caving in to fears
Or clinging to others
Or hiding my tears
Standing up on my own
Finding out who I am
Seeing that it's not so scary
To live without a man
Realizing all of the healing
That still needs to come
More time alone to honor me
To heal ~ To grow ~ To be okay
To find my way
Alone

Grieve

this too shall pass...

Grieve and feel the sorrow
For the one you've lost today
But worry not about the soul
Who's gone back home to stay

Remember all the memories
As they fill your mind
But do not have regrets or doubts
Or feel you've been left behind

As you walk through the stages of your loss
As tragic as it may seem
Know that an angel has just been reborn
In the world of hopes and dreams

Heartache

Gazing at the midnight sky
Hidden tears I cannot cry
Wishing stars falling down
Lonely beauty all around
Glimmers of the havest moon
Cast a sloft glow in my room
Enough to spy the empty space
Where once I laid in his embrace
I whisper prayers to give me peace
while angels rock my soul to sleep
The nights are long, yet the day is bright
Oh how my aching heart delights
To see a glimmer of the sun
And know a new day has begun
Moonlight shadows cast aside
Dreary dreams for now abide
Nightmares blinded by the light
Oh how I hope I'm healed by night

To Thy Own Self Be True

I struggle to cope, but really it seems
That trying to hard only dampens my dreams
So I welcome the hardships, I take what they teach
For the lessons I learn make my dreams within reach

Always remaining true to myself
Despite the commotion that weighs on my health
Will keep me connected to truth, love, and light
That shines from within me like a star in the night

Guiding my spirit, my soul ever last
That calls to my angels, my friends from time past
Feeling their love and comforting peace
That passes through me to others in need

A gift of healing
A prayer of hope
To Thy Own Self Be True
This is how I must cope

Live For The Moment

The past is just a place I've been
While the future is yet to be
And here and now I am writing this poem
And that is what matters to me

For although I may have memories
That plays throughout my mind
I know what counts most is the moment I'm in
And right now I am thinking in rhyme

I could sit and ponder the future
And worry of what is in store
But that has never served me well
The present holds enough to explore

Life is an exciting mystery
And our thoughts hold the key
It is our choice to have joy right now
If we let the past and future just be

Today

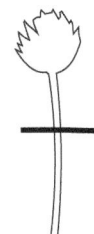

Today I will be content with all that comes my way
I will trust that there's a higher force
to help me through my day

Today I will think loving thoughts towards everyone I see
I will trust that all who cross my path
were sent as a gift to me

Today I will not crave for things or wish for better times
I will trust that where I am today
has been planned by one divine

Today I will not worry of decisions I must make
I will trust that as I need to know
I will be shown which path to take

Today I will take a moment to close my eyes and pray
and picture showers of love and peace
washing over the world today

I will trust that my prayers make a difference
and as sure as the flowers grow
for every loving thought I have a seed of peace will sow

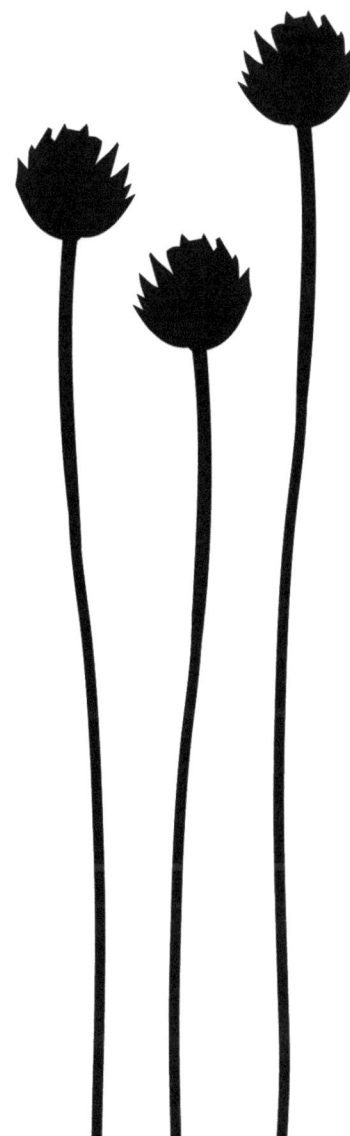

Believing in your dreams
as crazy as it seems
carries a force
that keeps you on course
until what you believe
you receive

Angel Dance

On the clouds little angels ride
On the merry go round of dreams

From one to the next there spirits dance
Spreading angels dust with their wings

Softly and slowly like sweet newborn smiles
The glittery powder sheds grace from the skies

Healing the hearts and hushing the cries
As on the clouds little angels ride

Miracles

Miracles happen
One is happening now
I feel the spirit of love
Love is behind all miracles

Love heals all things
It is healing now
I feel the spirit of compassion
Compassion is behind true love

Compassion unites humanity
It is uniting now
I feel the spirit of kindness
Kindness is behind compassion

Kindness fills the heart
Hearts are filling now
I feel the spirit of miracles
Miracles are behind kindness

Miracles happen
One is happening now
I feel the spirit of love
Love is behind all miracles

Love

Compassion

Kindness

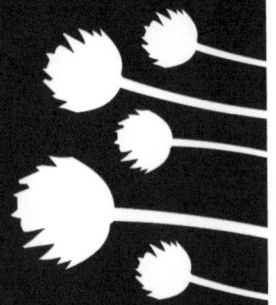

Dream

There is joy in sitting still
Long enough to ponder
And find that little childish place
That lets our minds go yonder

In that spot we find ourselves
A bit more open and true
To let our dreams dance around
Sparking our spirits a new

From this spark, a flame ignites
A passion in our hearts
And we all know about passionate dreams
No one can tear them apart

Beautiful

It's beautiful how you love me
Like a river running free
While stormy waters raise the river's edge
Your love flows ever deep

It's beautiful how you kiss me
Like thunder in the night
While lightning sparks the midnight sky
Your kiss my soul en' lights

It's beautiful how you hold me
Like an oak tree in the breeze
Like gusty winds shed branches gone weak
Your embrace sets my worries free

It's beautiful how you love me
Like the way that I love you
While all my dreams lie in your hands
Your love is my dream come true

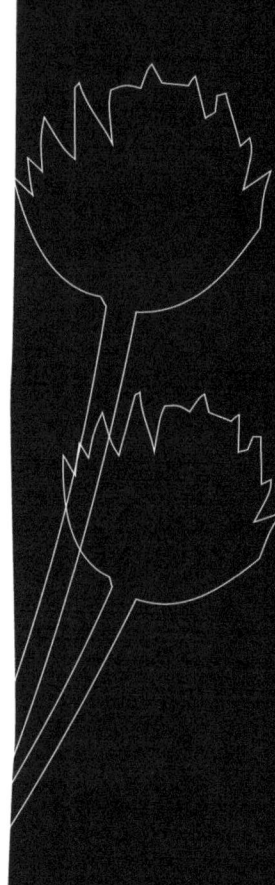

The Embrace

As I slip my arms around you
Reality melts away
My fears decrease to nothing
As I receive your love
In your embrace
I know I can change the world
And I love who I am
Your sweet words heal my spirit
Your eyes sing a lullaby to my soul
Calmness washes over me
It fills me so deeply with your love
That mine runs over
So I can give again freely
Without taking away from my spirit
Your embrace has rejuvenated me

Quite Like That

Is it like a whirlwind
rushing to and fro
Or could it be like a mountain
Mighty topped with snow
Maybe just a simple view
Stars upon the night
Or possibly a dolphins song
Echoing through oceans so bright
The laughter of a baby
A puppy kiss on the cheek
Sipping lemonade on the porch
Fuzzy slippers on my feet

Fluffy buttery pancakes
Maple syrup eggs and toast
Swaying on a tree swing
that hangs from a whispering oak
I cannot quite place the feeling
but I feel it when you're near
It is soft and sweet warm and safe
blissfully happy and dear
Maybe it's the feeling
of two hearts becoming one
Their spirits dancing to the beat
of a life that's just begun
This feeling is like a fairytale
but indeed it is a fact
It's like all of these things
that bring wonder and joy
Yes, it's quite like that

An Honorable Man

An honorable man seeks to be compassionate towards all and knows that judging others hurts his own spirit

An honorable man does not seek revenge on those who wrong him rather he shows his true strength by walking away

An honorable man recognizes the beauty and strength women were instilled with, he respects them as Queen's

An honorable man will reach out when he is downhearted and knows he must speak from his heart about what troubles him

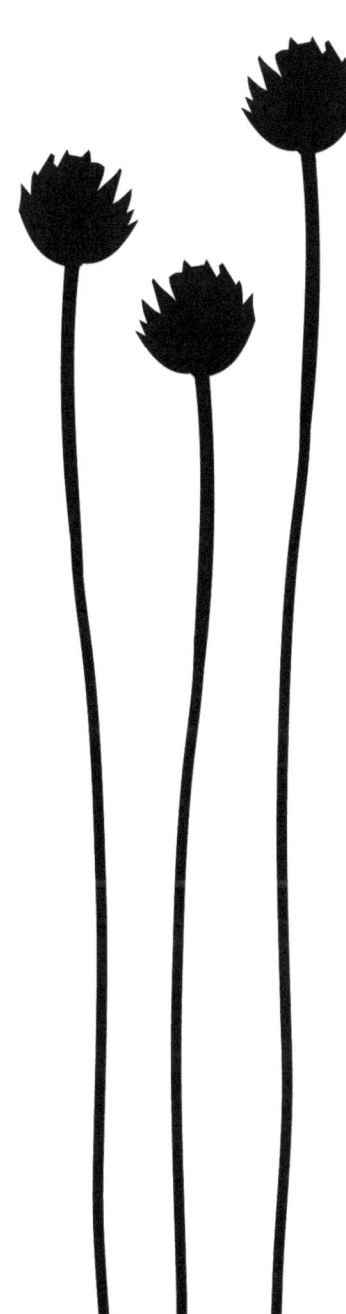

An honorable man knows his true warrior nature and protects his clan from harm, he knows when to battle and when to step back

An honorable man enjoys children and remembers the struggles of his youth, he teaches by example not harsh words

An honorable man does not deny his fears rather he faces them showing his courage

An honorable man holds his tongue when angry knowing the damage can cut deep into the hearts of those he loves if he does not

An honorable man will fail at being honorable time and time again but he will always keep trying, that is what makes him truly honorable

By God's Grace

I thank you Lord for all your love
I give my life to you
I know you see things I cannot
and know just what to do
So please guide me and show me
as each day unfolds
No sooner or later
just as I must know
I trust in you and release my fears
my burdens, guilt and stress
Replace these fears
with your comfort and love
My mind could use a rest

AMEN

Motherhood

The Perfect Mother

A loving mother watches me
and smiles at all I do
A brave mother holds me when
I feel afraid or blue
A concerned mother listens and nods
as my problems I confide
A smart mother always knows
when I try to tell a lie
A pretty mother puts on her smile
as she greets me at the door
An ambitious mother cleans the messes
cooks and much much more
A silly mother tries the new dances
to be a little more like me
A crabby mother comes around
when she needs her morning coffee
A fair mother says I'm sorry
when she is being a bit too strict
and even when I am mean to her
she never gets too ticked
I thought my mother was perfect
as perfect as mothers can get
until she told me a secret
that I never will forget

She sat me down and spoke these words
in a voice filled with love:

"I'm not as perfect as you think
I have help from up above
I make mistakes the same as you
and I even sometimes feel afraid
I get mad and I cry and at times even lie
it's okay that's just how we were made
By not being perfect we learn lots of things
and God planned it exactly that way
That's why he gave us tomorrows
to start a fresh new day!"

Now that I know my mother is not perfect
it makes her all the more perfect to me
Now when I make a mistake I know
I'm just being how I was made to be

Queen Mom

As she watches her children grow
Old Mom has many places to go
Running here and there
to meet all their cares
rain, or shine, or snow
Her job never ends you see
no time to sit and sip tea
Cleaning and scrubbing
for the family she's loving
that's the way her life has to be
The kids leave messes galore
they yell at mom and don't do their chores
Whining and fussing
and occasional cussing
and constantly saying their bored
But wait something's not right
the house it looks a fright

The dishes are piled
and moms lost her smile
and dinner is nowhere in sight
What's this, mom wants a break?
She's packed her bags and is leaving at eight?!
Despite the plea's
mom really leaves
with all their lives at stake
Finally mom comes back
she's ready to face the slack
But the kids have done chores
and even some more
and tell mom to go take a nap
When mom wakes she thinks it's a dream
the kids being nice and the house is still clean
Then the kids give a kiss
to the mother they missed
Old Mom has just become Queen!

Ode To My Life

Five times the chaos
Five times the fun
Five times the laundry
that never gets done

Five times the messes
the cooking the dishes
Five times the laughter
the singing the wishes

Five hugs goodbye
as they leave for school
Five kids arguing
with all of my rules

Five times the treasures
to hang on my walls
Five times the trips
to the local mall

Five times the worry
Five times the tears
Thats worth five goodnight kisses
from my five little dears!

My Little Angel

~ Arielle Nina ~ May 12th 1988

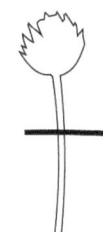

Each day and each night
You surround me with love
As you grow stronger
I thank God above
You have brought me hope
With your innocence and grace
In my heart there's a special path
Which only you can trace
Your smile is like diamonds
Your heart is like gold
The two finest things in the world
I've been told
You've given me courage
And my dreams you've made true
You've moved me to do things
I never could do
You are my child
My pride and my joy
The love that we share
Can never be destroyed

Wish On A Star
~ Johnathan Anthony ~ April 6th 1990

My second child
my first little boy
He brings me laughter
love and joy

He fills my world
with bright sunny smiles
His heart stretches on
for hundreds of miles

I watch him in wonder
as he grows
I am amazed everyday
at the things that he knows

My heart bursts with pride
for this child of mine
He's the wish on a star
that makes my life shine

Sealed With A Kiss

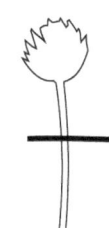

~ Brett Matthew ~ February 5th 1993

You came out quiet not a single noise
My sweet little baby my cuddly boy

The nurses were worried and wondered just why
For never does a baby come out with no cry

I knew you had something special inside
A gift that God gave you, a gift you can't hide

I've felt it and seen it and others have too
Your calm peaceful spirit is a miracle like you

I'm proud and excited to have such a child
I love how you laugh and I love how you smile

I love how you always try to make me feel loved
By saying nice things and giving me hugs

You're a treasure to me and I promise you this
I'll love you forever, sealed with a kiss!

Sweet Little Beaner Boo
~ Serena Rose ~ July 6th 1994

Little angels sang that night
as a little girl was born
Soft and sweet she came to me
my life she did adorn

Her face could not be cuter
had I planned it out that way
and her precious smile and twinkling eyes
are as sweet as angels at play

My little girl reminds me
that dreams they do come true
Serena Rose, you are my dream
My sweet little Beaner Boo!

Last But Not Least
~ Michael Edward ~ September 7th 1995

You beat the odds
Your will was strong
You came into my world
right where you belong

Through my sickness I held you
I held you close
you melted my pain
you gave me hope

You were the last of five
a gift from above
you were last but not least
for you healed me with love!

Just For Fun

Twinkle Twinkle

As I walked through the store with my 4yr old son shopping for dinner that night, he began to chant a familiar song but something just wasn't quite right.

People began to stare at us looking shocked by what they heard. That's when I noticed my sons little song, he was changing all the words.

"Twinkle, twinkle poopy star," he sang throughout the store. I began to feel flustered and nervous as I frantically fled to the door.

When we reached our car I told my son that his song was not ok. He just looked in my eyes and said to me, "Have a poopy day!"

Mortified, I rushed right home wondering what I should do. My once sweet little boy threw off his coat and yelled, "Take off my poopy shoes!"

That is when I knew I had a problem, a big one I could tell. My son had discovered "potty talk" and was mastering it quite well.

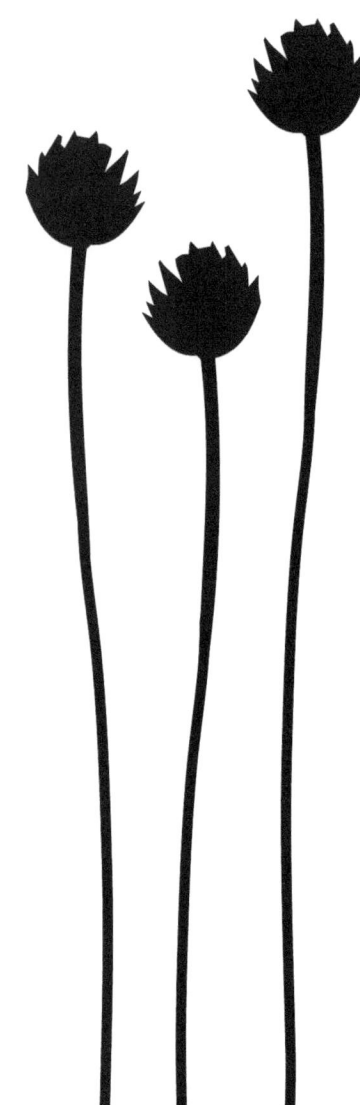

I sat him down for a serious talk and explained my point of view. I told him that using that word in a song is something he never should do.

Later that night as I went to bed I felt everything would be fine. He had not said the "word" the rest of the day. I think I nipped it just in time.

The next day when I took my son to the doctor I was nervous he'd say it once more but, as we waited to be called by the nurse he just quietly played on the floor.

I began to relax since once again my son was his sweet little self, when the nurse called his name I was full of pride as he put the toys back on the shelf.

We went with the nurse to the Doctor's room and then to my dismay, she told me my little guy needed his shots before we left that day.

As she left the room I knew I had to prepare him for the blow, so I quietly explained that he needed a shot that would help him be healthy and grow.

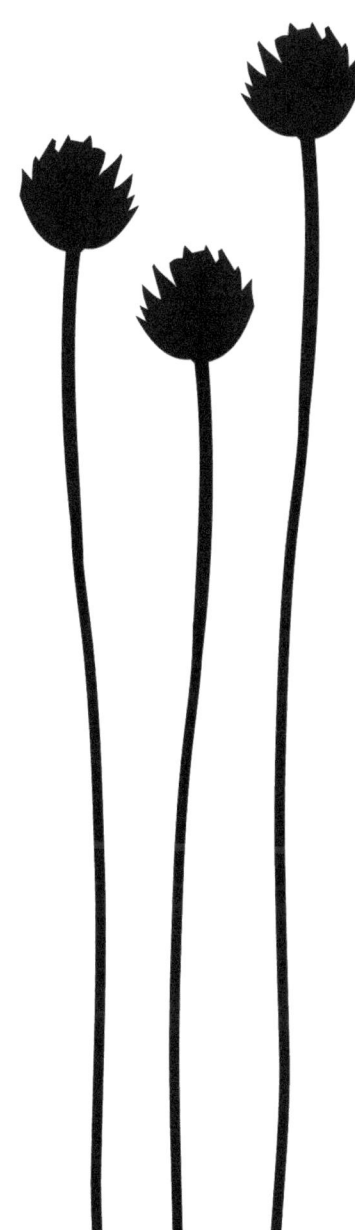

My son began to yell and cry, kicking and carrying on, so I picked him up to sooth him and promised it wouldn't take too long.

This did not help a single bit, he cried harder than before, and I knew I had to calm him down before the doctor came through the door.

I felt hopeless and my heart was heavy, for his sadness was too much to bear, I knew what it was that I had to do, and at that moment I really didn't care.

I bent down and whispered in his ear a song I knew he'd like "Twinkle, twinkle poopy star" I sang to my little tike.

His tears turned into laughter, as the doctor came inside and I kept right on singing our little song for his feelings meant more than my pride.

That Doctor, he may think I'm crazy but the truth of the matter is this, when it comes to soothing a screaming child, it takes more than a little kiss!

The End

The Snow Day

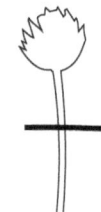

One day I awoke to frost on the windows and felt the chilled that filled the air. I thought of the long cold winter days ahead of me I must bear.

As I sorted through all of the winter clothes, a memory crept into my mind, of all the wet clothing, the sloshy boots, and lost mittens we never find.

I thought of the frustration of dressing the children, preparing them for the cold, and when they come home how they track snow through the house no matter how many times they are told.

I thought of scrapping the car windows, and shoveling all of the snow, sanding the sidewalk, winterizing the car, getting stuck and needing a tow.

The winter blues began setting in as I thought of the hassles ahead, and to think it is only the beginning, oh how the winter I dread!

I sat with my coffee and tried to relax, but then to my surprise, the news caster announced that school's been closed. The tears welled in my eyes.

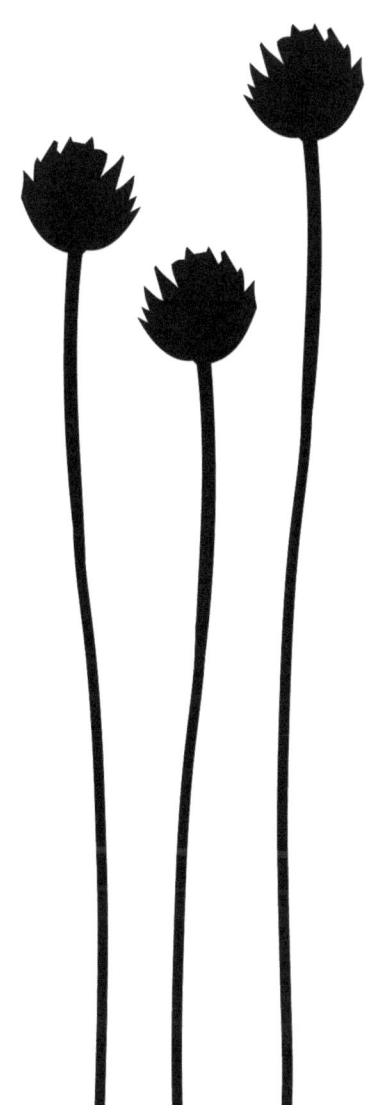

All the kids home for the entire day? Whatever will I do!? It is bad enough to deal with the cold, but now a SNOW DAY TOO!!!

Then all the children began to arise, they ran to the window and stared. When they saw all the snow, their eyes lit up, not a worry or care.

They turned to me in excitement and asked if they could go out to play, so I bundled them up and dug out the sleds and sent them on their merry way.

I watched them from the window jumping in the snow and felt a slight flutter in my heart as I saw their happiness aglow.

Suddenly, I heard a little cry and saw my youngest still sitting inside. He was watching them play through the window with a look of fear in his eyes.

I went to him and picked him up and hugged him oh so tight. I told him I would go out with him and everything would be alright.

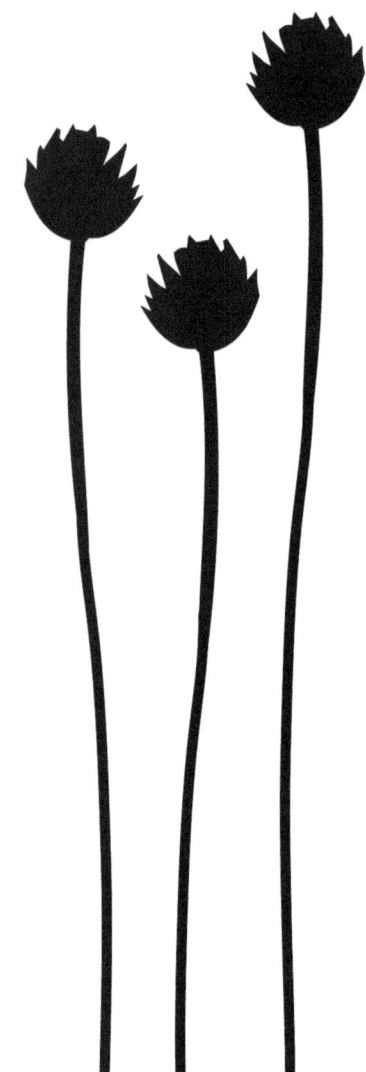

As we went outside he clung to me still doubtful and afraid. Then the other children yelled for us to come see what they had made.

We walked over to the children and their standing by a tree, was the biggest snowman I had ever seen, with a smile filled with glee.

In excitement my son jumped to the ground and ran to get a closer peek, and then my oldest child lifted him up to kiss "Frosty" on his cheek.

They all played together the rest of the day making snow forts and angels galore, as I was reminded that nothing is so bad if you look at the good a bit more.

The End

www.ingramcontent.com/pod-product-compliance
Lightning Source LLC
Chambersburg PA
CBHW041529220426
43671CB00002B/37